Brown v. Board of Education:
The Road to a Landmark Decision

Lorin Driggs

Reader Consultants

Brian Allman, M.A.
Classroom Teacher, West Virginia

Cheryl Norman Lane, M.A.Ed.
Classroom Teacher
Chino Valley Unified School District

iCivics Consultants

Emma Humphries, Ph.D.
Chief Education Officer

Taylor Davis, M.T.
Director of Curriculum and Content

Natacha Scott, MAT
Director of Educator Engagement

Publishing Credits

Rachelle Cracchiolo, M.S.Ed., *Publisher*
Emily R. Smith, M.A.Ed., *VP of Content Development*
Véronique Bos, *Creative Director*
Dani Neiley, *Associate Editor*
Fabiola Sepulveda, *Series Designer*
Alette Straathof, *Illustrator, pages 6–9*

Image Credits: Cover Getty Images/Bettmann; p4 Library of Congress [LC-USF346-031873-D]; p11 Gerrit Groenewegen ; p16 National Archives; p17 bottom Archives and Manuscripts, Library of Virginia; p19 Library of Congress [LC-DIG-ppmsc-00199]; p20 Newscom/World History Archive; p21 Library of Congress [LC-DIG-nclc-00525]; p22 Library of Congress [LC-DIG-ds-130145]; pp25–26 Getty Images/Carl Iwasaki; p27 top Newscom/Everett Collection; p27 bottom Library of Congress [LC-DIG-ds-11820]; p29 United States Department of Agriculture; all other images from iStock and/or Shutterstock

This book may not be reproduced or distributed in any way without prior written consent from the publisher.

5482 Argosy Avenue
Huntington Beach, CA 92649
www.tcmpub.com

ISBN 978-1-0876-1552-3
© 2022 Teacher Created Materials, Inc.

The name "iCivics" and the iCivics logo are registered trademarks of iCivics, Inc.

Table of Contents

A Difficult Topic 4

Jump into Fiction:
   Moving Forward 6

The Legacy of Slavery 10

President Lincoln's Proclamation 14

Three Big Steps Forward 16

A Big Step Backward 20

Brown v. Board of Education
   Makes History 26

Glossary 30

Index 31

Civics in Action 32

A Difficult Topic

Let's face it. Some topics are really hard to talk about, even with your friends and your teachers. Some things are even hard for families to talk about. But when something makes people uncomfortable, it may be something important to talk about.

Racial **segregation** is one of those topics. *Segregation* means separation. For a long time in the past, Black children could not go to school with white children. Black and white people were separated in other ways, too.

1938 segregated classroom in Arkansas

Segregation was a choice that white people in some states made. They made their choice into laws. It was against the laws for Black people to do some of the same things as white people. If Black people tried, they could go to jail. They were also harmed and hurt.

Segregation has a difficult and complicated history. Tracing the history of segregation shows how laws, ideas, attitudes, people, and even countries can change for the better.

21st-century classroom

Jump into Fiction

The Legacy of Slavery

A court case called *Brown v. Board of Education* made racial segregation in schools illegal in the United States. That was in 1954. But to tell that story, we have to go back even further—more than 300 years earlier.

Slavery was legal from the earliest days of America's history. Racial segregation has its roots in this practice.

Slave traders **kidnapped** Africans and brought them to the United States. The traders enslaved them and sold them. Enslaved Africans were in a new place, far from home. Even if they escaped, where could they go? White people saw them as property. They forced enslaved people to work without pay.

In the South, cotton was a **cash crop**. Cotton was grown on huge areas of land called **plantations**. Plantation owners used enslaved workers so they could save money. They were able to spend less on production costs and make more of a profit. The conditions were awful, and enslavers treated Black people in **brutal** ways. Enslaved people resisted this treatment. They bravely tried to make their lives better.

Plantation owners forced enslaved people to pick cotton.

A Dangerous Trip

From 1500 to 1866, slave traders took 10 to 12 million people from Africa. Traders took them on ships across the Atlantic Ocean. This journey was known as the *Middle Passage*. The ships had terrible conditions. Thousands of enslaved people died.

Over time, some Americans changed their ideas about slavery. By 1804, slavery was against the law in the North. Some of the laws meant to bring slavery to a gradual end, so it did not happen right away. But things were different in the South. Growing cotton was more profitable than ever. Plantation owners wanted enslaved people to keep working.

Meanwhile, the United States was growing and expanding in the West. Southern enslavers wanted to bring enslaved people to the new territories. Northern lawmakers wanted to keep slavery out of the West.

Disputes between the North and the South finally broke apart the country. In 1861, seven Southern states **seceded**. That means they separated from the United States so they could form a new country. Soon, four more states joined them. The result was the start of the **Civil War**. The North fought to prevent Southern states from leaving. The South fought to defend its way of life, including slavery.

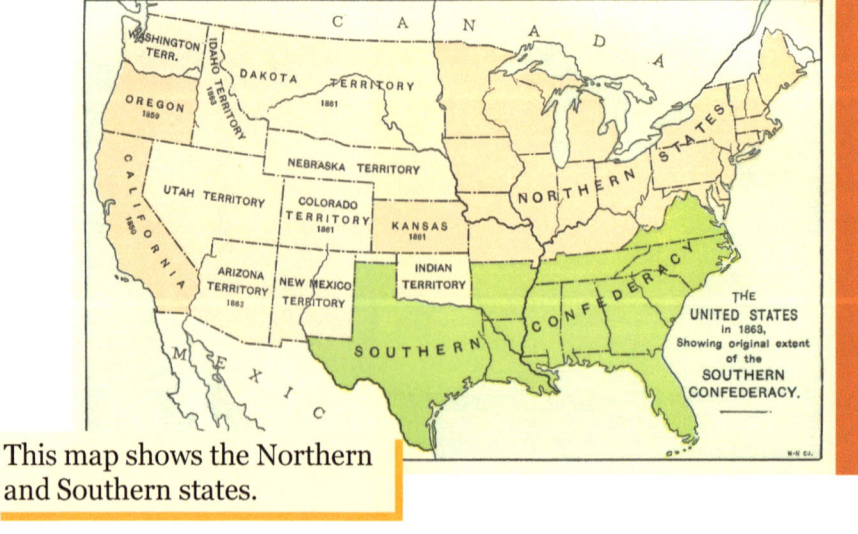

This map shows the Northern and Southern states.

illustration of an 1864 Civil War battle

The Anti-Slavery Movement

Around 1830, an official **movement** emerged. This group of Americans wanted to end slavery. They were called *abolitionists*. The name comes from the word *abolish*, which means "to do away with or outlaw something." Black people who had escaped slavery and white people were part of this movement.

President Lincoln's Proclamation

Abraham Lincoln was president during the Civil War. In 1863, he took a bold step. He issued an order called the **Emancipation Proclamation**. *Emancipation* is another word for freedom. His order did not immediately end slavery. But it opened the doors to further legislation.

The Civil War lasted from 1861 to 1865. Eventually, the North won. And the Southern states were part of the United States again.

President Lincoln reads the text of the Emancipation Proclamation with his Cabinet members.

illustration of the day the Emancipation Proclamation was declared

The war had ended, but Black people still faced many challenges. A lot of white people, especially in the South, would not accept that slavery had ended. This type of thinking was a problem.

There was also the issue of rights. The **Constitution** is the basis of all laws in the United States. Former enslaved people were not yet considered **citizens** under the Constitution. Because of that, they did not have the rights that other people did, such as the right to vote. The road to equality lay ahead. It would be a long, hard journey.

Three Big Steps Forward

The only way to change legal rights was through the Constitution. So, the U.S. government took three big steps to fix that. They made amendments to the Constitution. An amendment is a change.

The Thirteenth Amendment

In 1865, a change was made to the United States Constitution. It was called the Thirteenth Amendment. It made slavery illegal. This change legally prohibited people from being enslaved in the United States.

The Fourteenth Amendment

The Fourteenth Amendment was passed in 1868. It said that Black people were citizens. It also said that they must have the same rights as other citizens.

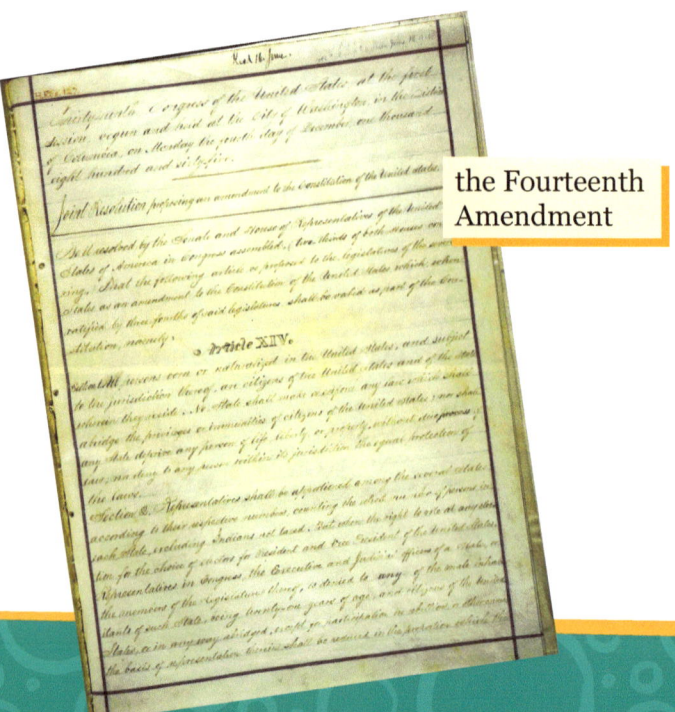

the Fourteenth Amendment

The Fifteenth Amendment

In 1870, the Fifteenth Amendment became a law. It granted Black men the right to vote.

These amendments gave Black people the same rights as other citizens. These changes were a good start. Still, they weren't enough. Slavery had done a lot of damage.

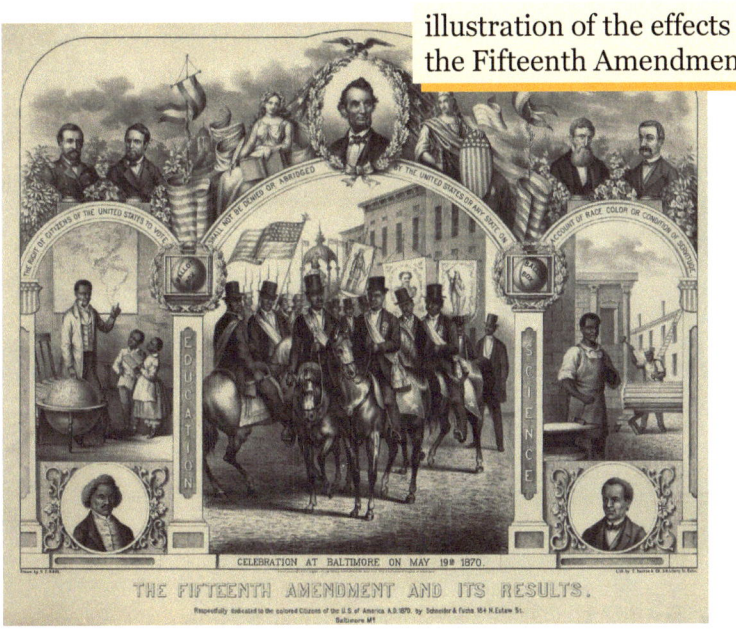

illustration of the effects of the Fifteenth Amendment

The Right to Vote

The Fifteenth Amendment gave Black men the right to vote. But no women had the right to vote. This changed in 1920. Women gained the right to vote under the Nineteenth Amendment. Yet, many Black women were still excluded because of segregation.

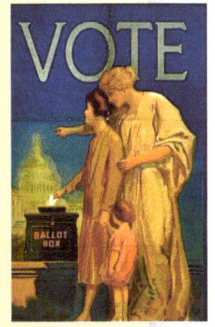

The Constitution had been changed to give rights to Black people. But the changes to the Constitution didn't change everything.

Slavery from the past haunted the present. Many white people did not want to have Black friends or neighbors. They did not want their children to share classrooms with Black children. Segregation prevented people from interacting or from getting to know each other.

Segregation did not happen everywhere, but in many states, segregation of races was required by law. Here are some examples. Black people could not go to the same schools as white people. They could not eat in restaurants with white people. Black people had to sit in separate parts of movie theaters, buses, and trains. They had to use separate restrooms and water fountains. White and Black people could not marry each other. In some areas, they could not even live in the same neighborhoods.

1910 geography class in a Black school in Washington, DC

This 1940 bus station has segregated waiting rooms.

Jim Crow Laws

Some states passed laws that kept Black people segregated from white people. These were called *Jim Crow laws*. Jim Crow was the name of a fictional character. It represented a negative view of Black men. Up until the 1960s, signs that said "Whites Only" or "Colored" could be seen in many public places.

A Big Step Backward

In 1892, Homer Plessy, a Black man, took a seat in a white-only railcar in Louisiana. He was arrested. He had broken a state law requiring separate facilities for Black and white people in public places. Plessy challenged that law in court. He claimed that the Fourteenth Amendment gave Black people "equal protection of the laws." The **Supreme Court** ruled that it was legal to have "separate but equal" places for white people and Black people. This meant that it was legal to *separate* Black and white people. They just had to provide *equal* resources.

In states that allowed segregation, the "separate but equal" ruling was a harsh blow for Black people. It was not fair to Black people. It made many people angry.

Rosa Parks Takes a Seat

In 1955, in Montgomery, Alabama, Black people had to sit in the backs of city buses. The law said that only white people could sit in the front. Rosa Parks chose to not obey the law. She was arrested. Her action led to a **boycott**. Black people stopped taking buses. That eventually led to a Supreme Court decision that stopped **discrimination** on buses, trains, and planes.

The separate places for Black people were rarely equal to places for white people. This was especially true in schools. Schools for Black children received less money than schools for white children. The buildings were run-down. School buses needed repair. There were not enough books or other supplies. And Black teachers were paid less than white teachers.

Black schoolhouse in Anthoston, Kentucky, 1916

The NAACP's Crusade

Black people came together to continue to advocate for the equality and respect they deserved. They would not settle for less. The National Association for the Advancement of Colored People (NAACP) took up their causes.

The NAACP was formed in 1909. One of its goals was to create "equal educational opportunities" for all children in every state. They also wanted equal public school **expenditure**. They thought the amount of money spent should be the same for Black and white children. To accomplish this, they knew they needed to fight for people's **civil rights**.

In 1935, Donald G. Murray wanted to be a lawyer. The University of Maryland Law School would not let him enroll. Why? He was Black. The NAACP took his case and won. In 1938, Murray graduated from that law school.

A Mixed Group

The founders of the NAACP were a diverse group of Black and white men and women. They were sociologists, writers, religious leaders, teachers, social workers, and more.

McLaurin attends class at the University of Oklahoma in 1948.

In 1948, George W. McLaurin, a Black man, applied to the all-white University of Oklahoma. At first, the university refused. A court said the school had to admit him. However, the university made rules for McLaurin. He could not be near white students in classrooms. He had to use separate areas in the library, cafeteria, and restrooms. The NAACP took his second case. It went all the way to the Supreme Court. The NAACP lawyer argued that these rules violated the Fourteenth Amendment. In 1950, the Court agreed.

Five Cases Become One

There were other victories in court. But one hard fact remained. "Separate but equal" said that segregation was still legal.

The NAACP was looking for the chance to have that practice struck down forever. It found that chance in 1951. In Kansas, seven-year-old Linda Brown had to walk six blocks to catch the bus. The bus then took her to an all-Black school. The nearest school to Linda's home was for white students only. It was not necessarily better than the all-Black school. But her parents and others said that even if the schools were "equal," segregation itself was wrong. Parents in Delaware were upset with the inequal conditions at Black schools compared to the white schools. One parent wanted her child to be able to ride the white bus that passed her house every school day. In Virginia, both students and parents were unhappy with the school's terrible conditions and wanted that to change. In Washington, DC, parents said that the all-Black school was not equal to the white schools. Their children's school was overcrowded and run-down. In South Carolina, lawyers for Black parents argued that the concept of segregation was harming children.

The NAACP combined these five cases into one. It reached the Supreme Court under the name *Brown v. Board of Education*.

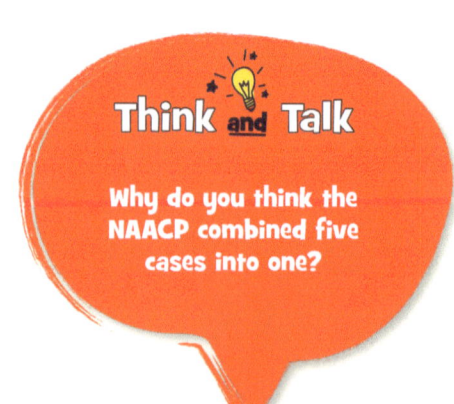

Think and Talk

Why do you think the NAACP combined five cases into one?

the students (from left: Vicki Henderson, Donald Henderson, Linda Brown, James Emanuel, Nancy Todd, and Katherine Carper) and parents whose cases are represented in *Brown v. Board of Education*

Brown v. Board of Education Makes History

The NAACP lawyers argued the case before the Supreme Court. They talked about how far Black students had to travel. They talked about unequal conditions in school. They said segregation could harm Black children's "hearts and minds in a way unlikely ever to be undone."

In 1954, *Brown v. Board of Education* made history. The Supreme Court justices agreed with the NAACP lawyers. They said that a good education was "a right which must be made available to all on equal terms." They declared that "separate but equal . . . has no place in the field of public education."

Segregation based on race in schools was finally illegal. It was a huge victory. But it was only the beginning.

Linda Brown (left) with her parents and sister

How would schools be **integrated**? Who would be responsible? In 1955, the Supreme Court issued another decision. It was called *Brown v. Board of Education II*. It said schools must end segregation "with all deliberate speed." But this was a long process. It did not happen automatically. There was still work to do.

integrated classroom in 1954

From NAACP Lawyer to Supreme Court Justice

Thurgood Marshall was the lead lawyer in the *Brown v. Board of Education* case. In 1967, he was appointed to the Supreme Court by President Lyndon B. Johnson. This made Marshall the first Black justice on the Supreme Court.

The Fight Continues

The Supreme Court's decision was monumental. It stated that "'separate but equal' has no place" in public education. The decision gave great momentum to the civil rights movement. Across the country, and especially in the South, Black people demanded equal rights.

The civil rights movement took many forms. Black people sat peacefully in white-only restaurants. They refused to use services that discriminated against them. Often, they were attacked and put in jail. But they did not give up. And, they continued enrolling their children in schools. Some schools did not want to desegregate. At times, the U.S. government sent in federal troops to enforce the law.

In 1963, more than 250,000 people of all races marched in Washington, DC. It was a show of unity and strength. Dr. Martin Luther King Jr. spoke. It is one of the most famous speeches in American history. "I have a dream," he said. He described his dream of equality and peace.

The next year, the United States passed the Civil Rights Act of 1964. Discrimination based on race, color, religion, or national origin was now against the law.

Brown v. Board of Education was a tipping point for many people. It helped change society in the United States. These changes continue today.

view of the March on Washington crowd at the National Mall

Mendez v. Westminster

About seven years before *Brown v. Board of Education*, a case about segregation in schools went to federal court. The case originated in Orange County, California. At the time, Mexican American children could not attend white schools. The court ruled that segregation of Mexican American students was unconstitutional. Thurgood Marshall was also involved in this case.

Glossary

boycott—the process of people joining together with others and refusing to deal with a person or a business as a way of protesting or forcing changes

brutal—cruel and violent

cash crop—a crop that is grown for the purpose of selling it and making a profit

citizens—people who legally belong to a country and have the rights and protection of that country

civil rights—basic rights given by the government to every citizen

Civil War—a war between two groups of states in the United States

Constitution—the document that contains all the basic laws of the United States

discrimination—the practice of unfairly treating a person or group of people differently from other people or groups of people

Emancipation Proclamation—an order by President Abraham Lincoln to free the enslaved people in 10 states

expenditure—an amount of money that is spent on something

integrated—allowed all types of people to participate or be included; not segregated

kidnapped—took away a person by force

movement—an organized effort working toward a desired end

plantations—large areas of land used to grow crops

seceded—separated from a nation or state and became independent

segregation—the practice or policy of keeping people of different races, religions, etc. separate from one another

Supreme Court—the highest court in the United States, which decides whether a law is legal according to the Constitution of the United States

Index

abolitionists, 13

Brown v. Board of Education, 10, 24–29

Brown, Linda, 24, 26

Brown v. Board of Education II, 26

Civil Rights Act of 1964, 28

Civil War, 12, 14

Constitution, 15–16, 18

Emancipation Proclamation, 14–15

Fifteenth Amendment, 17

Fourteenth Amendment, 16, 20, 23

Jim Crow laws, 19

Johnson, Lyndon B., 27

King, Dr. Martin Luther, Jr., 28

Lincoln, Abraham, 14

Marshall, Thurgood, 27, 29

McLaurin, George W., 23

Montgomery, Alabama, 20

Murray, Donald G., 22

NAACP (National Association for the Advancement of Colored People), 22–24, 26–27

Nineteenth Amendment, 17

Parks, Rosa, 20

Plessy, Homer, 20

Thirteenth Amendment, 16

Washington, DC, 18, 24, 28

Civics in Action

The history of civil rights in the United States is complicated. It has not always moved toward progress, and it can be difficult to talk about. But it is important to know about the past to understand the present. Many people and groups worked and sacrificed to make things better and improve civil rights. You can learn more about these people, groups, and events.

1. Choose a person, organization, or important event from the book.

2. Research your chosen subject.

3. Choose a project (such as a poster, brochure, or newspaper article) to spread the news of what happened. Create your project.

4. Share your work!

www.ingramcontent.com/pod-product-compliance
Lightning Source LLC
Chambersburg PA
CBHW041506010526
44118CB00001B/35